THE JPS B'NAI MITZVAH TORAH COMMENTARY

Mase'ei (Numbers 33:1–36:13)
Haftarah (Jeremiah 2:4–28; 3:4)

Rabbi Jeffrey K. Salkin

The Jewish Publication Society · Philadelphia
University of Nebraska Press · Lincoln

INTRODUCTION

News flash: the most important thing about becoming bar or bat mitzvah isn't the party. Nor is it the presents. Nor even being able to celebrate with your family and friends—as wonderful as those things are. Nor is it even standing before the congregation and reading the prayers of the liturgy—as important as that is.

No, the most important thing about becoming bar or bat mitzvah is sharing Torah with the congregation. And why is that? Because of all Jewish skills, that is the most important one.

Here is what is true about rites of passage: you can tell what a culture values by the tasks it asks its young people to perform on their way to maturity. In American culture, you become responsible for driving, responsible for voting, and yes, responsible for drinking responsibly.

In some cultures, the rite of passage toward maturity includes some kind of trial, or a test of strength. Sometimes, it is a kind of "outward bound" camping adventure. Among the Maasai tribe in Africa, it is traditional for a young person to hunt and kill a lion. In some Hispanic cultures, fifteen year-old girls celebrate the *quinceañera*, which marks their entrance into maturity.

What is Judaism's way of marking maturity? It combines both of these rites of passage: *responsibility* and *test*. You show that you are on your way to becoming a *responsible* Jewish adult through a public *test* of strength and knowledge—reading or chanting Torah, and then teaching it to the congregation.

This is the most important Jewish ritual mitzvah (commandment), and that is how you demonstrate that you are, truly, bar or bat mitzvah—old enough to be responsible for the mitzvot.

What Is Torah?

So, what exactly is the Torah? You probably know this already, but let's review.

The Torah (teaching) consists of "the five books of Moses," sometimes also called the *chumash* (from the Hebrew word *chameish*, which means "five"), or, sometimes, the Greek word Pentateuch (which means "the five teachings").

Here are the five books of the Torah, with their common names and their Hebrew names.

- **Genesis (The beginning), which in Hebrew is Bere'shit (from the first words—"When God began to create").** Bere'shit spans the years from Creation to Joseph's death in Egypt. Many of the Bible's best stories are in Genesis: the creation story itself; Adam and Eve in the Garden of Eden; Cain and Abel; Noah and the Flood; and the tales of the Patriarchs and Matriarchs, Abraham, Isaac, Jacob, Sarah, Rebekah, Rachel, and Leah. It also includes one of the greatest pieces of world literature, the story of Joseph, which is actually the oldest complete novel in history, comprising more than one-quarter of all Genesis.
- **Exodus (Getting out), which in Hebrew is Shemot (These are the names).** Exodus begins with the story of the Israelite slavery in Egypt. It then moves to the rise of Moses as a leader, and the Israelites' liberation from slavery. After the Israelites leave Egypt, they experience the miracle of the parting of the Sea of Reeds (or "Red Sea"); the giving of the Ten Commandments at Mount Sinai; the idolatry of the Golden Calf; and the design and construction of the Tabernacle and of the ark for the original tablets of the law, which our ancestors carried with them in the desert. Exodus also includes various ethical and civil laws, such as "You shall not wrong a stranger or oppress him, for you were strangers in the land of Egypt" (22:20).
- **Leviticus (about the Levites), or, in Hebrew, Va-yikra' (And God called).** It goes into great detail about the kinds of sacrifices that the ancient Israelites brought as offerings; the laws of ritual purity; the animals that were permitted and forbidden for eating (the beginnings of the tradition of kashrut, the Jewish dietary laws); the diagnosis of various skin diseases; the ethical laws of holiness; the ritual calendar of the Jewish year; and various agricultural laws concerning the treatment of the Land of Israel. Leviticus is basically the manual of ancient Judaism.

> Numbers (because the book begins with the census of the Israelites), or, in Hebrew, Be-midbar (In the wilderness). The book describes the forty years of wandering in the wilderness and the various rebellions against Moses. The constant theme: "Egypt wasn't so bad. Maybe we should go back." The greatest rebellion against Moses was the negative reports of the spies about the Land of Israel, which discouraged the Israelites from wanting to move forward into the land. For that reason, the "wilderness generation" must die off before a new generation can come into maturity and finish the journey.

> Deuteronomy (The repetition of the laws of the Torah), or, in Hebrew, Devarim (The words). The final book of the Torah is, essentially, Moses's farewell address to the Israelites as they prepare to enter the Land of Israel. Here we find various laws that had been previously taught, though sometimes with different wording. Much of Deuteronomy contains laws that will be important to the Israelites as they enter the Land of Israel—laws concerning the establishment of a monarchy and the ethics of warfare. Perhaps the most famous passage from Deuteronomy contains the *Shema*, the declaration of God's unity and uniqueness, and the *Ve-ahavta*, which follows it. Deuteronomy ends with the death of Moses on Mount Nebo as he looks across the Jordan Valley into the land that he will not enter.

Jews read the Torah in sequence—starting with Bere'shit right after Simchat Torah in the autumn, and then finishing Devarim on the following Simchat Torah. Each Torah portion is called a parashah (division; sometimes called a *sidrah*, a place in the order of the Torah reading). The stories go around in a full circle, reminding us that we can always gain more insights and more wisdom from the Torah. This means that if you don't "get" the meaning this year, don't worry—it will come around again.

And What Else? The Haftarah

We read or chant the Torah from the Torah scroll—the most sacred thing that a Jewish community has in its possession. The Torah is written without vowels, and the ability to read it and chant it is part of the challenge and the test.

But there is more to the synagogue reading. Every Torah reading has an accompanying haftarah reading. Haftarah means "conclusion," because there was once a time when the service actually ended with that reading. Some scholars believe that the reading of the haftarah originated at a time when non-Jewish authorities outlawed the reading of the Torah, and the Jews read the haftarah sections instead. In fact, in some synagogues, young people who become bar or bat mitzvah read very little Torah and instead read the entire haftarah portion.

The haftarah portion comes from the Nevi'im, the prophetic books, which are the second part of the Jewish Bible. It is either read or chanted from a Hebrew Bible, or maybe from a booklet or a photocopy.

The ancient sages chose the haftarah passages because their themes reminded them of the words or stories in the Torah text. Sometimes, they chose *haftarah* with special themes in honor of a festival or an upcoming festival.

Not all books in the prophetic section of the Hebrew Bible consist of prophecy. Several are historical. For example:

The book of Joshua tells the story of the conquest and settlement of Israel.

The book of Judges speaks of the period of early tribal rulers who would rise to power, usually for the purpose of uniting the tribes in war against their enemies. Some of these leaders are famous: Deborah, the great prophetess and military leader, and Samson, the biblical strong man.

The books of Samuel start with Samuel, the last judge, and then move to the creation of the Israelite monarchy under Saul and David (approximately 1000 BCE).

The books of Kings tell of the death of King David, the rise of King Solomon, and how the Israelite kingdom split into the Northern Kingdom of Israel and the Southern Kingdom of Judah (approximately 900 BCE).

And then there are the books of the prophets, those spokesmen for God whose words fired the Jewish conscience. Their names are immortal: Isaiah, Jeremiah, Ezekiel, Amos, Hosea, among others.

Someone once said: "There is no evidence of a biblical prophet ever being invited back a second time for dinner." Why? Because the prophets were tough. They had no patience for injustice, apathy, or hypocrisy. No one escaped their criticisms. Here's what they taught:

> God commands the Jews to behave decently toward one another. In fact, God cares more about basic ethics and decency than about ritual behavior.
> God chose the Jews *not* for special privileges, but for special duties to humanity.
> As bad as the Jews sometimes were, there was always the possibility that they would improve their behavior.
> As bad as things might be now, it will not always be that way. Someday, there will be universal justice and peace. Human history is moving forward toward an ultimate conclusion that some call the Messianic Age: a time of universal peace and prosperity for the Jewish people and for all the people of the world.

Your Mission—To Teach Torah to the Congregation

On the day when you become bar or bat mitzvah, you will be reading, or chanting, Torah—in Hebrew. You will be reading, or chanting, the haftarah—in Hebrew. That is the major skill that publicly marks the becoming of bar or bat mitzvah. But, perhaps even more important than that, you need to be able to teach something about the Torah portion, and perhaps the haftarah as well.

And that is where this book comes in. It will be a very valuable resource for you, and your family, in the b'nai mitzvah process.

Here is what you will find in it:

> A brief **summary** of every Torah portion. This is a basic overview of the portion; and, while it might not refer to everything in the Torah portion, it will explain its most important aspects.
> A list of the **major ideas** in the Torah portion. The purpose: to make the Torah portion real, in ways that we can relate to. Every Torah portion contains unique ideas, and when you put all

of those ideas together, you actually come up with a list of Judaism's most important ideas.

> Two **divrei Torah** ("words of Torah," or "sermonettes") for each portion. These *divrei Torah* explain significant aspects of the Torah portion in accessible, reader-friendly language. Each *devar Torah* contains references to **traditional** Jewish sources (those that were written before the modern era), as well as **modern** sources and quotes. We have searched, far and wide, to find sources that are unusual, interesting, and not just the "same old stuff" that many people already know about the Torah portion. Why did we include these minisermons in the volume? Not because we want you to simply copy those sermons and pass them off as your own (that would be cheating), though you are free to quote from them. We included them so that you can see what is possible—how you can try to make meaning for yourself out of the words of Torah.

> **Connections:** This is perhaps the most valuable part. It's a list of questions that you can ask yourself, or that others might help you think about—any of which can lead to the creation of your *devar Torah.*

Note: you don't have to like everything that's in a particular Torah portion. Some aren't that loveable. Some are hard to understand; some are about religious practices that people today might find confusing, and even offensive; some contain ideas that we might find totally outmoded.

But this doesn't have to get in the way. After all, most kids spend a lot of time thinking about stories that contain ideas that modern people would find totally bizarre. Any good medieval fantasy story falls into that category.

And we also believe that, if you spend just a little bit of time with those texts, you can begin to understand what the author was trying to say.

This volume goes one step further. Sometimes, the haftarah comes off as a second thought, and no one really thinks about it. We have tried to solve that problem by including a **summary** of each haftarah, and then a mini-sermon on the haftarah. This will help you learn how these sacred words are relevant to today's world, and even to your own life.

All Bible quotations come from the NJPS translation, which is found in the many different editions of the JPS TANAKH; in the Conservative movement's *Etz Hayim: Torah and Commentary;* in the Reform movement's *Torah: A Modern Commentary;* and in other Bible commentaries and study guides.

How Do I Write a *Devar Torah?*

It really is easier than it looks.

There are many ways of thinking about the *devar Torah.* It is, of course, a short sermon on the meaning of the Torah (and, perhaps, the haftarah) portion. It might even be helpful to think of the *devar Torah* as a "book report" on the portion itself.

The most important thing you can know about this sacred task is: *Learn* the words. *Love* the words. Teach people what it could mean to *live* the words.

Here's a basic outline for a *devar Torah:*

"My Torah portion is (name of portion)_____,
    from the book of _____ , chapter

_____.

"In my Torah portion, we learn that_____
    (Summary of portion)
"For me, the most important lesson of this Torah portion is (what
    is the best thing in the portion? Take the portion as a whole;
    your *devar Torah* does not have to be only, or specifically, on the
    verses that you are reading).
"As I learned my Torah portion, I found myself wondering:
    > *Raise a question that the Torah portion itself raises.*
    > *"Pick a fight"* with the portion. Argue with it.
    > *Answer a question* that is listed in the "Connections" section of
      each Torah portion.
    > *Suggest a question to your rabbi* that you would want the rabbi
      to answer in his or her own *devar Torah* or sermon.

"I have lived the values of the Torah by _____
(here, you can talk about how the Torah portion relates to your
own life. If you have done a mitzvah project, you can talk about
that here).

How To Keep It from Being Boring
(and You from Being Bored)

Some people just don't like giving traditional speeches. From our per-
spective, that's really okay. Perhaps you can teach Torah in a different
way—one that makes sense to you.

- Write an "open letter" to one of the characters in your Torah portion. "Dear Abraham: I hope that your trip to Canaan was not too
  hard . . ." "Dear Moses: Were you afraid when you got the Ten
  Commandments on Mount Sinai? I sure would have been . . ."
- Write a news story about what happens. Imagine yourself to
  be a television or news reporter. "Residents of neighboring cities were horrified yesterday as the wicked cities of Sodom and
  Gomorrah were burned to the ground. Some say that God was
  responsible . . ."
- Write an imaginary interview with a character in your Torah portion.
- Tell the story from the point of view of another character, or a mi-
  nor character, in the story. For instance, tell the story of the Garden of Eden from the point of view of the serpent. Or the story
  of the Binding of Isaac from the point of view of the ram, which
  was substituted for Isaac as a sacrifice. Or perhaps the story of
  the sale of Joseph from the point of view of his coat, which was
  stripped off him and dipped in a goat's blood.
- Write a poem about your Torah portion.
- Write a song about your Torah portion.
- Write a play about your Torah portion, and have some friends act
  it out with you.
- Create a piece of artwork about your Torah portion.

The bottom line is: Make this a joyful experience. Yes—it could
even be fun.

The Very Last Thing You Need to Know at This Point

The Torah scroll is written without vowels. Why? Don't *sofrim* (Torah scribes) know the vowels?

Of course they do.

So, why do they leave the vowels out?

One reason is that the Torah came into existence at a time when sages were still arguing about the proper vowels, and the proper pronunciation.

But here is another reason: The Torah text, as we have it today, and as it sits in the scroll, is actually *an unfinished work*. Think of it: the words are just sitting there. Because they have no vowels, it is as if they have no voice.

When we read the Torah publicly, we give voice to the ancient words. And when we find meaning in those ancient words, and we talk about those meanings, those words jump to life. They enter our lives. They make our world deeper and better.

Mazal tov to you, and your family. This is your journey toward Jewish maturity. Love it.

THE TORAH

❖ Mase'ei: Numbers 33:1–36:13

This is the final portion in the book of Numbers. It tells us about the various places that the Israelites encamped during their wandering in the wilderness.

As the Israelites prepare to enter the Land of Israel, God tells Moses about the boundaries of the land. God commands Moses to set aside cities for the Levites to dwell in. There must be cities of refuge among those cities—special places to which people who have killed someone unintentionally can flee, in order to escape the vengeance of a family member of the deceased.

The portion ends with a revisiting of the case of the daughters of Zelophehad, but this time with a new twist—they must marry within their own tribe, so that their inheritance will stay within the larger family.

Summary

- The Torah portion contains a list of the forty-two places at which the Israelites stopped during their wanderings. It forms an extensive, intricate itinerary (33:1–49). (Interesting piece of trivia: when these verses are chanted in the synagogue, the chanter uses the same tune that is used at the Song of the Sea.)
- More geography! The boundaries of the Land of Israel are established. (34:1–12)
- There are procedures for dealing with those who unintentionally kill others. They can flee to cities of refuge in order to be safe from the victim's relatives who will be seeking vengeance. (35:1–34)
- Once again, the daughters of Zelophehad push God on an issue of social and communal justice. They had earlier challenged God and Moses on the issue of being able to inherit from their father (Numbers 27). Now, the tribal leaders object that if they marry outside their tribe, their inheritance would pass to their husbands' tribes. God decrees that heiresses must marry within their own tribes. (36:1–12)

The Big Ideas

› **Jewish history is a journey, and it is crucial to remember all the places that the Jews have lived.** Sure, the Torah account of all those places might seem a little tedious and repetitive; over and over again, the verses tell us: *va-yisu va-yachanu,* they set out from . . . they camped in . . . . But that is an essential piece of Jewish history—wandering from one place to another, staying there for a while, and then moving on, when necessary. That is also the way that our own lives unfold. We stay in one place for a while (literally and figuratively), we move on, we have adventures, things go well, or not so well—and we grow.

› **There is no Judaism without a love of the Land of Israel. That would account for the careful detail with which the biblical author describes the boundaries of the land.** The boundaries as described in these verses actually go as far south as present-day Egypt; as far north as cities in present-day Lebanon; and as far as Damascus, which is in present-day Syria! At a time when politicians and everyday people debate what the borders of the State of Israel should be, this biblical "map" does not and cannot reflect current reality. The Jewish love for the Land of Israel does not necessarily rely on the precise biblical boundaries of the land.

› **Judaism requires both justice and mercy.** Yes, Judaism takes murder very seriously. But it also recognizes that not all killing of another person is deliberate homicide. Accidents happen, and while they are tragic those accidents neither require nor merit vengeance. The Torah recognizes the reality that people sometimes kill each other and that there must be a system in place for dealing with homicides—both intentional and unintentional.

› **God responds to human need and human circumstances.** The book of Numbers is filled with complaints, both to Moses and to God, and this latest plea from the daughters of Zelophehad is the final "complaint." God responds to the fear that other tribes would inherit the daughters' inheritances by telling them that they must marry within their own tribe. How is that good? Isn't it just a further restriction on the daughters and on their marital choices? Yes it is, but, luckily for them, their tribe was quite large so we assume there were many marriageable men. The Torah is making it clear: the tribe—the larger family that is at the core of the Jewish people—is sacred.

Divrei Torah
GOD'S GPS SYSTEM

GPS systems (or Google Maps) are among the modern world's greatest inventions. Think of it: back in the "old days," there were very few ways to figure out where you were going. You could look at a road map and try to figure it out, or you could ask someone for directions and hope they knew what they were talking about. Now, all you have to do is type the address of your destination and in a nanosecond you will find the route.

Here is something else about many of these GPS systems—and it is either cool or weird. The GPS stores every address that you have entered. Just scroll through the GPS, and you will find a list of every place that you have gone—or, at the very least, every place that you have used the GPS to find.

That's how this Torah portion works as well. It lists every single place that the Israelites camped in, showing their route to the Land of Israel. (Years ago, a kid who became bar mitzvah actually traveled this route in Israel. Very cool.)

Now, you might think that this is the most boring portion of the Torah—just a list of ancient place names, about as exciting as reading, well, a GPS. Why does the Torah have to include this long list? And, to be fair, there are other accounts of journeys in the Torah that have different place-names, or sometimes are in a different order.

So, what's the big deal? What can we learn from this laundry list of places?

First, the whole chapter has a hidden message: God's love for the Jewish people endures, in spite of everything. A midrash teaches: "It is like the case of a king whose son was ill. He took him to a certain place to cure him. On their return journey, his father began to recount all the stages, saying: "Here we slept; here we cooled ourselves; here you had a headache." So God said to Moses: "Tell them all the places where they provoked Me."

God remembers every step on the Jewish people's journey. It's like your parents keeping old photographs of you from when you were growing up. You were not always an easy child. But your parents like looking at the photographs and remembering, and hopefully you do too.

Second, what goes for the ancient Israelites goes for us. Each of us is a product of a journey that is both ancient and modern. Rabbi Arthur Green offers an example: "They journeyed from Berditchev and camped in Hamburg. They sailed from Hamburg and landed in Ellis Island. They journeyed from Ellis Island and camped on Rivington Street. They journeyed from Rivington Street and camped in the Bronx, on the Grand Concourse. They journeyed from the Grand Concourse and settled in Teaneck."

You didn't just get where you are by accident. You were led. Are you grateful?

"IT WAS JUST AN ACCIDENT!"

This has happened to you. You were hanging out, doing "nothing"—and you: (a) dropped and broke your cell phone; (b) broke a window; or (c) spilled a soft drink onto your mother's laptop computer. Whatever it is, you're in big trouble. And all you can say is: "I didn't mean to do it! It was just an accident!"

But what if (God forbid) a man or woman accidentally ran over someone with a car? The official term for that kind of thing is "manslaughter." What would the person do? Today the answer is easy, even though the situation is tragic. He or she would report this terrible thing to the police, and apologize to the family. There might or might not be criminal charges. But one thing's pretty sure: the family of the dead person would not come after the accidental killer and try to kill him or her. At least, we hope not.

That is the situation that this Torah portion describes: the accidental killer. In ancient times, if someone (even accidentally) killed someone, there was always the danger that the dead person's relatives would pursue the "killer." So, the Torah provides six cities of refuge, to which an accidental killer could flee so that there would be no vengeance taken against him or her.

Now, it's not as if the accidental killer gets a totally free pass. The Torah makes it clear: If you hit someone with a stone or wooden tool and that person dies, then you are a murderer. You should have known what was going to happen. Similarly, if you hate another person and you push that person, or throw something at that person, then you are assumed to have acted with malice, and you are a murderer. And, yes—a family member of the deceased could come after you in cases of intentional homicide.

Terrible, right? Perhaps, but this was a major change from the other societies of the ancient world. In those societies, if you killed someone, you could just pay a fee to the bereaved family, and call it a day. Not in the Torah. According to Bible scholar Moshe Greenberg: "In biblical law, the taking of life cannot be made up for by any amount of property, nor can any property offense be considered as amounting to the value of a life."

But the Torah is also saying that there is a difference between outright murder, which the Ten Commandments prohibit, and killing. Society is responsible for making sure that the accidental killer is safe from vengeance. The great medieval sage Maimonides teaches: "The court is obligated to remove all obstacles to cities of refuge so as not to delay one who is fleeing to one of them. The width of a road to a city of refuge should not be less than thirty-two cubits." "Refuge, Refuge" was written at all crossroads so that the perpetrator of manslaughter would recognize the way and turn there. Keep in mind that the person who flees to the city of refuge is not escaping punishment. He must stay there and not go home until a specified period of time has elapsed.

The bottom line: Judaism believes in justice. But justice is not the same as revenge. Intention matters and the punishment should fit the crime. Sometimes we do bad things we didn't mean to do, but there are consequences nonetheless.

Connections

➤ Why do you think that the places listed in this parashah are chanted in the same tune as the song that the Israelites sang when they crossed the sea (Exodus 15)? How are those two experiences the same?

➤ Why do you think it is important to record the Israelites' journey in such detail? What can we learn from this?

➤ Do you know the places where your own family (and your grandparents, or great-grandparents) lived? Have you ever visited those places? What was that experience like?

➤ What do you think of the differences between murder and killing? Do you agree with those differences? What are the implications of this teaching for political refugees—those who have not even killed someone, but are searching for freedom?

THE HAFTARAH

❖ Mase'ei: Jeremiah 2:4–28; 3:4

This is the second of the three *haftarah* that are read in synagogue between 17 Tammuz and Tisha b'Av. Jeremiah relates that God is having serious trouble believing the Jewish people have betrayed the covenant with God, thus putting themselves in serious danger.

First, they totally forgot about God. And then, they went and worshiped idols. It just doesn't make sense, God says. But, wait a second, God says, maybe they still do remember me. Maybe all is not lost.

God My Father, God My Companion

Okay, let's admit it: not everyone is in love with the whole "God and Israel" marriage thing (see last week's haftarah). First of all, marriages back in ancient times weren't always so great, especially for wives. And second, if you've never been married (or even had a serious boyfriend or girlfriend), the whole comparison is probably lost on you.

Fine. Luckily, the final words of this haftarah give us another way of thinking about our relationship with God. Actually, two other ways. Try them on.

"Just now you called to Me, 'Father! You are the Companion of my youth'" (3:4). Looking at the first half of that biblical passage, one way is to think of God as Father. Many people don't like attributing the male gender to God, so let's just cut to the chase here: it's not about God as Father, really; it's about God as Parent. Rabbi Richard Levy writes: "How would you like your mother to be? How would you like your father to be? Your parents have the potential to be that way, but God is that way now. The kind of parent-love you want . . . it's there in God."

While God might be the ideal parent, relationships between parents and kids constantly grow and evolve. Sometimes, that relationship means anger—which comes from both sides in fact. You've slammed your share of bedroom doors in your time, haven't you—swearing that you're never going to talk to your parents again? The Jews did that, too, when they got angry with God. Even Moses did it. Seeing into the future at how the great sage Rabbi Akiva would ultimately suffer at the hands of the Romans, Moses cried out: "This is the Torah, and this is its reward?" And just as you ultimately made up with your parents (and they, with you), we can ultimately make up with God, as well.

The second half of the biblical passage gives us a second way to look at our relationship with God: "Companion of my youth." Being God's friend—that's a very sweet and trusted metaphor. Jews actually sing about it on Yom Kippur: "We are your beloved; you are our friend." Abraham was called "the friend of God" (in fact, that is how Abraham is known in Muslim lore).

There are many dimensions of friendship worth mentioning: hanging out, sharing interests, admiration, trust. But what's beautiful in the verse is how it plays out: "You are the Companion *of my youth.*" It's like having a friend, but one you've been out of touch with for a while. Maybe you went to different schools, or different camps—and, suddenly, you rediscover each other, and the friendship is revived.

That's why this haftarah ends on such a joyous note. Yes, the relationship with God had been estranged. The Jews had abandoned the covenant and worshiped idols. But God knew that the people would come back, and they would remember what it was like when they were young, back in the days of Abraham and Sarah, and Moses. . . .

The Jews and God would be back together again—just like old times.

❖ Notes

CPSIA information can be obtained
at www.ICGtesting.com
Printed in the USA
LVHW111159271118
598383LV00009B/370/P